Dolly Parton

Keep On Dreaming

Keepsake Gift Book

A Gift For:

_____

From:

_____

Prayer is not a formal affair,

it's more a come-as-you-are.

—Dolly Parton

Dolly Parton, 2012 *Joyful Noise* premiere.

I always count my blessings more than I count my money. I don't work for money, never did.

—Dolly Parton

A rhinestone shines just as good as a diamond.

—Dolly Parton

Never ignore your roots,

your home, or your hair.

—Dolly Parton

Dreams are of no value if they're not equipped with wings!

—Dolly Parton

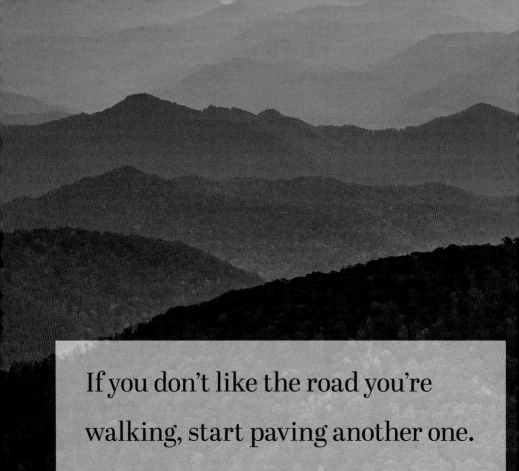

If you don't like the road you're walking, start paving another one.

—Dolly Parton

Being a star just means that you just find your own place, and that you shine where you are.

—Dolly Parton

Dolly Parton, 2019 MusiCares Person of the Year Gala.

When I got somethin' to say,

I'll say it.

—Dolly Parton

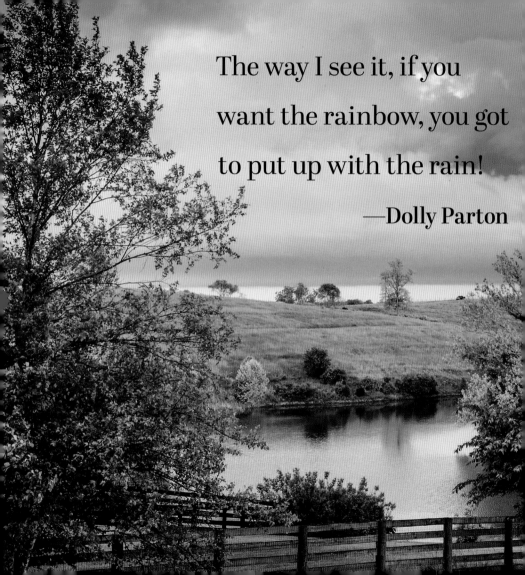

The way I see it, if you want the rainbow, you got to put up with the rain!

—Dolly Parton

People say, 'How you stay looking so young?' I say, 'Well, good lighting, good doctors, and good makeup.'

—Dolly Parton

I'm not offended by all the dumb blonde jokes because I know I'm not dumb—and I'm not blonde either.

—Dolly Parton

Dolly Parton, 2006 Academy Awards.

Storms make trees

take deeper roots.

—Dolly Parton

Don't get so busy making a living that you forget to make a life.

—Dolly Parton

When someone shows me their true colors, I believe them.

—Dolly Parton

You'll never do a whole lot unless

you're brave enough to try.

—Dolly Parton

Find out who you are.

And do it on purpose.

—Dolly Parton

I have a strict policy that no one cries alone in my presence.

—Dolly Parton

I don't often lose my temper,

but I often have to see it.

—Dolly Parton

If I can hold God's attention, I can hold the world's.

—Dolly Parton

I think everyone should be allowed to be who they are, and to love who they love.

—Dolly Parton

Dolly Parton, 1995 Dixie Stampede Dinner Show.

I never tried quitting,

and I never quit trying.

—Dolly Parton

I'm the little engine that did.

—Dolly Parton

Dolly Parton in *Straight Talk*, 1992.

I make a point to appreciate all the little things in my life. I go out and smell the air after a good, hard rain. These small actions help remind me that there are so many great, glorious pieces of good in the world.

—Dolly Parton

Dolly Parton, 2022 Academy of Country Music Awards.

The only advice I'd give would be the advice I follow myself.

—Dolly Parton

Dolly Parton, CMT Flameworthy Awards, 2004.

If your actions create a legacy that inspires others to dream more, learn more, do more, and become more, then you are an excellent leader.

—Dolly Parton

I'm not going to limit myself just because people won't accept the fact that I can do something else.

—Dolly Parton

If you talk bad about country music, it's like saying bad things about my momma. Them's fightin' words.

—Dolly Parton

We cannot direct the wind,

but we can adjust the sails.

—Dolly Parton

After you reach a certain age, they think you're over. Well, I will never be over. I'll be making records if I have to sell them out of the trunk of my car. I've done that in my past, and I'll do that again.

—Dolly Parton

Dolly Parton, 1989.

I have to not harden my heart, because I want to stay open to feel things. So when I hurt, I hurt all over. And when I cry, I cry real hard. And when I'm mad, I'm mad all over. I'm just a person; I like to experience whatever the feeling is and whatever I'm going through.

—Dolly Parton

Dolly Parton, 1979.

I've had heartaches, headaches, toothaches, earaches, and I've had a few pains in the ass, but I've survived to tell about it.

—Dolly Parton

Dolly Parton, 2016 Academy of Country Music Awards.

Dolly Parton Keep On Dreaming is an original work, first published in 2025 by Fox Chapel Publishing Company, Inc.
All rights reserved. No part of this publication may be reproduced, stored in a retrieval
system or transmitted, in any form or by any means, electronic, mechanical, photocopying,
recording or otherwise, without the prior written permission of the copyright holders.

This book is an independent and unauthorized publication. No endorsement or sponsorship by—and no affiliation
with—Dolly Parton, *Joyful Noise,* or any of the companies that offer authorized products and services relating to
Dolly Parton are claimed or suggested. All references in this publication to intellectual property owned by Dolly
Parton and her affiliated companies are for the purpose of identification, commentary, criticism, and discussion.
Purchasers of this book are encouraged to buy the authorized products and services related to Dolly Parton.

Images from Shutterstock.com: Tinseltown (3); Featureflash Photo Agency (5, 23); shutt2016 (6-7); Bart Sherkow (9);
Jack Fordyce (11); Weidman Photography (13); Kathy Hutchins (15, 21, 47, 63); DFree (17); Alexey Stiop (18-19); Smileus
(24-25); Joe Seer (27); David P Baileys (30-31); Carl Beust (39); Wirestock Creators (41); ju_see (42-43); SueST (55).

Images from Alamy.com: Allstar Picture Library Limited (29); PictureLux/The Hollywood
Archive (33, 35, 37, 45, 49); Album (51, 53); Pictoral Press Ltd (57, 59, 61);

ISBN 978-1-4971-0561-4

The Cataloging-in-Publication Data is on file with the Library of Congress.

To learn more about the other great books from Fox Chapel Publishing, or to find a retailer near you,
call toll-free 800-457-9112, or visit us at www.FoxChapelPublishing.com.

You can also send mail to:
903 Square Street
Mount Joy, PA 17552.

We are always looking for talented authors. To submit an idea, please send a brief inquiry to
acquisitions@foxchapelpublishing.com.

Printed in China

First printing